THE STARRY MESSENGER

Pitt Poetry Series

Ed Ochester, Editor

THE STARRY MESSENGER

George Keithley

University of Pittsburgh Press

The publication of this book is supported by a grant
from the Pennsylvania Council on the Arts

Published by the University of Pittsburgh Press, Pittsburgh, Pa., 15260
Copyright © 2003, George Keithley
Manufactured in the United States of America
Printed on acid-free paper
10 9 8 7 6 5 4 3 2 1
ISBN 0-8229-5816-3

For Clark and Noël Brown

Contents

I

PASSION

The fact of our imperfect understanding should not be allowed to feed our anxiety and so increase the need to control. Rather, our studies should be inspired by a more ancient, but today less honored, motive: a curiosity about the world of which we are part. The rewards of such work are not power but beauty.

Gregory Bateson

1

His father Vincenzo—a musician—had fallen out of favor
with the only nobles who might hire him, ever.
Hot-tempered, quick to curse, he drank each cup
of his disgrace among his family. Daily
a red-faced rage frightened his wife and son.

About the boy: Born in Tuscany
and christened Galileo Galilei,
when he grew into his thick body
and blunt speech
his hair, like his father's, had a fiery luster.

Never a scholar
though inquisitive from his first breath
(his mother vowed)
in time he became a loud quarrelsome youth
contrary, she thought, to his tender nature.

Children of shrewd merchants and comfortable landowners
called him—to his face—a conceited ass
though his parents were ashamed of their poverty.

2

In the neighborhood. In the shadows of the abbey.
"Bastard!"
Boys spit on his knobby hands.
"Dunce!"
Until he adapted a metronome to time the human pulse.

A ready brawler,
he fought them
often weeping
before he was struck

for he lived in fear
of the vicious kick
or sharp rock.

He too hit hard
and if his strength failed him he flailed on
but blinded by tears
he was beaten to his knees
in the street. In the schoolyard.

3

When he sold his design for a military compass
he presented the money to his mother.

4

Because his genius was for dynamics
he invented a hydrostatic balance.

5

Finding the frequency of its return depends upon the length
of the object departing
("Does this apply . . . ?")
he devised the first pendulum for a clock.

6

However, tutors found him unteachable:
"He thinks with his fists!"
He was denied a scholarship to Pisa.

"Others may kiss a man's cloak.
I labor like an ox—
No rest from the yoke."

7

Nobles, a few, took notice. Churchmen, too.

Night and day he educated his eye
to discern the exact progress
of objects in motion,
whether linear or orbital.

Bristling at each rebuke,
he advanced swiftly
with a passionate will
because he improved on the efforts of modest mechanics.

"A prepared mind works the most potent magic
this side of our dreams. And death."
So thought an enlightened Cardinal del Monte.
And, yes, it was he
who commended the anxious youth to the Duke of Tuscany.

"Yet, one wonders, can he learn accommodation?
Or is he, alas, more trouble than he's worth?"

First, in Pisa, *il Profesore* teaches
practical mathematics, though he laments
his "pauper's income." Now, in Padua,
he instructs, tinkers, observes, experiments.

By candlelight he reads forbidden authors:
Doctor Copernicus and the astral magician
Giordano Bruno—each believes the earth
orbits the sun—while he writhes with ambition.

The state of knowledge? Copernicus is condemned.
Bruno won't recant; he raves in prison.
Kepler is dreamy, conscientious—what
will *that* get him?—quiet about his vision.

Among his students Galileo prefers the poor,
whose learning, like his own, has been hard-won:
"Curiosity requires a stubborn heart."
Among the faculty he favors none . . .

"Devout sheep, frightened by a daring thought!"
Envied, loathed, shunned, he curses his colleagues:
"My brothers? But they're blind and mute! Maggots,"
he calls the lay scholars. "Mental pygmies."

Few among the religious orders—Jesuits,
Dominicans, monks or priests—escape his scorn:
"Buffoons! Venom-spitting greedy vultures!
Ungrateful villains, evil, unfit to be born!

Their intellects are antique: silver-scrolled.
What use are such ornate vessels?" he asks.
"They hold no rare wine. Nor did they ever.
You might as well piss in these empty flasks!"

Tempering his tongue, he concedes: "They cherish ancient
ways. And what can *I* teach anyone that might
comfort a troubled soul? Better to lie
with your beloved in your arms tonight!

Because love obeys no law but its own,
each heart may be a heretic. The mind?
Never! Its one worthy work is the pursuit
of that hidden truth we cannot comprehend."

1

In the pit of his being sits an obese belligerent boy
gnawing on his sleeve
weeping
because he comprehends the divine
architect of this world and its myriad marvels
also designed
—but why?—
a fearful child
unworthy of love.

2

He invents the glass thermometer.
Purely for its chemical behavior
he prefers wine to water
(rising, descending)
in the slender vertical cylinder
of the stem.

3

Rumor tells us
he's fascinated by the study of falling bodies.
His lectures attract eager minds from Paris, Leiden, London.

4

Among admirers
he appears vain, jealous, self-righteous:
"Let's laugh at the stupidity of the mob," he urges.

5

When he discovers the path
of every projectile
is a parabolic arc
the mind's eye opens
and we believe
with the lark and the dove
in the curvature of time
and the incessantly shifting
shape of things to come.

6

Rumor tells us
he prefers wine to water.

Taught by his father
he plays the lute ably but sings off-key
in a boisterous voice.
Among admirers
he recites poems and swaps gossip.

No longer does he worship
God on his knees—
standing in the nave
of the cathedral he prays
with a breathless respect
to the deity he names,
Lord of Our Nights and Days.

7

Suddenly his first mistress is with child.

He hopes to amass a fortune by improving
on another's design for a nautical compass.

He invents an irrigation pump for desperate farmers.
He sells his intelligence to warlords, feuding armies.

8

However, for many years he publishes little
because he dreads the ridicule of his elders—

Not the rumors of debauchery (these he lives with)
but attacks upon his methodology and his faith.

Because he has not the humility of Copernicus.

Because he lacks the forthright grace
and the stumbling vulnerability of Kepler.

9

He shoulders his telescope to the top of the campanile.
"That ship cresting the horizon—already we identify its flag."

Merchants empty their purses for his labors—
"A marvelous instrument to protect our harbors!"

Left alone, he refines his lenses, rubs his eyes.
One night—soon—he will train them on the skies.

Everything begins with desire—
After she'd lit the little amber lamp
with an intricate turn of her wrist
he watched while she brushed her hair.

Why did this make him smile?
The lamplight on her arm and on her hair
like a river restless yet careful
to sustain its shimmering surface.

Later the curtains danced like skirts
young women wear to the market

and the room was cool when they awoke
in one another's arms
in the middle of the dark—

They'd left their window half-open
to hear a late summer rain falling
and falling, a shivering sound,
all night among the sweet plum trees.

October, 1609. As autumn turns the oak
beneath his roof vermilion
wood smoke clings to the tiles.
He longs for winter skies velvet black.

Charting the planets through their starry heaven
Galileo allows no fires in *his* house.
No heat—
no smoke or haze to obscure his vision.

In December he dismantles his telescope to replace
its most powerful lens.
The new image is less imposing
but more precise

and he enjoys two weeks of unobstructed sighting.
When a stiff pain grips his hip
he paces with a limp
or leans, all night, observing and writing.

By midnight his eyes burn and brim
with tears. Before dawn
the cold slows his blood.
His legs ache until they grow numb.

He wrings his fingers and they redden. Now he draws
his final sketch. Finished, he wags
both gnarled hands before his face.
"My lobsters," he laughs. "My claws . . . !"

In a beeswax candle the braided wick
is all but gone. Its flame
—a nervous blue—shivers
as he shifts a quilt across his back.

"Must I be blind," he asks, "to God's creation?
All intellect still cowers in its cell:
Are we forbidden to lift our gaze?
Isn't learning, like prayer, an act of devotion?"

6 ⋆ *His Fondness for Animals, His Fear of Pain,*
His Fabulous Appetite

Among people he's brusque—at best—yet he treats
animals with unfailing tenderness. In
particular his pet spaniels, spoiling them
with kitchen scraps for the pleasure
of their tongues lapping his stout fingers.
Bribing the balky truculent mule
with apples, beets, bits of honeycomb.
A blanket of Afghan wool for the colt.
There at the family villa in the hills,
scattering bread crumbs for the doves
on winter mornings (though sciatica
burns both his legs). And isn't *that*
where he designed a delicate glass device
—actually the first eyedropper—
to nurse his daughter's ailing cat?

Small wonder he has no appetite
for hunting game: "Worse than children
stalking shadows—it's all tedium
and terror. Hours of witless waiting.
For what? To shoot an arrow straight
through a hapless creature's throat." So,
grant him this—his compassion for
another's anguish as he perceives it:
An elk struck down in wind-swept grass.
Its agony—the last loveless cry
before death—sickens him, inducing
incontinence, fever and chills,
as if the pain were his own. Pity

no less real because it *never*
dissuades him from his copious dinner . . .

Tonight in a single sitting he devours
the flesh of two young pheasants. Plums.
Champignons in pasta, pine nuts, olives.
A sea bass boned then dressed with limes.
Breads baked in an Etruscan kiln . . .
All day the portly boar has been skewered
over blue-hot coals. Basted; turning
the russet brown of autumn leaves
and spiced apples. Now it's lifted
from the hissing pit and brought to table
on a huge platter trimmed with mint. Yes,
offer him this! While the fellow consumes
three full and succulent servings,
as dreadful guests do, he washes down
each one with your finest wine—*bless* you!

7 ⋆   *Writing in Her Diary, His Daughter Welcomes
the First Spring Rain Falling in the Hills*

When mother dances barefoot across the kitchen
the hem of her skirt sweeps the tile floor: *Whisk,
whisk!* Her feet fly. *Whisk, whisk!* Oh, but there's more.
Listen—Papa's laughing. Clapping. Hopping
about the parlor. How the table trembles!
He throws open the window and there he stands
singing full-throated like the entire cast
of maestro Monteverdi's *Orfeo.* Or
those tiers of white-robed choirboys (what delightful
little devils!) performing Easter Mass
at St. Mark's. In truth, he carries a tune
no better than his flop-eared mule braying
for breakfast. (Papa's voice alarms our cats;
they scoot for cover puling beneath my chair.)
Nevertheless he serenades us, yes,
and prances like a prince because this morning
(at last!) our plum orchard hears the rain begin.
Now from winter's gloom every glossy tree
unbends; its soul, seeking water, reaches
into the light and catches it with its green hands.

1

Galileo is astonished that a full-grown man might find himself
staring childlike at the evidence—simple, irrefutable—
which each day offers. As when he observes
the force which pumps blood through his veins
lifts the dawn
dripping from the canals of Venice,
surprising the doves with a sudden shower.

The sky clears—and what can he learn of the doves?
This flock aloft now in the light.
How they welcome the air, trust it, abandon themselves to it.

How they soar unburdened beneath the morning sun.

2

Nature asks us
what is matter?
Does energy travel
a continuous curve?

What creature, therefore,
truly knows peace?
Is ever at rest?

He watches fishermen
haul their catch
onto the dock—a web

of troubled abundance,
writhing, silver
sides swollen until

the purling net
sags, pulls apart,
pours its dazzle
flapping into the cart.

3

A man of no little faith,
he believes life is eternal
energy, boundless in body and soul,
as the sun ministers to the whispering city:

First it disperses shadows, then, dexterously
as a rose opens
it dries the stones
on the Piazza San Marco and they blaze like bronze!

It's daybreak and he's almost sober. Soon the pride
of the Cathedral—its carillon—will beckon
the faithful to matins. God, how he loves this hour!
Not the mist lifting in first light from the *laguna*
but the way the water wakes the lusty city
with a low voice—sultry and violent as hers—
while it wears the dawn like Dutch damask upon
the bodice of his mistress, no longer young, arranging
her hair; abundance rippling with each motion.
To hell with those who tell you the study of nature
is not the study of power! Galileo hears
the slow current shifting through the channel
of San Nicolo; in a moment the market—six hundred
tents and canvas stalls—will open its arms
to the harbor. Heaven and earth offer all
the cargo a man desires. Weighted with grain,
Arabian horses, gunpowder, lumber—teak
and cedar—opium, salt, Siberian furs,
stowaways in the hold too frightened to speak,
ships rock at anchor on the glittering water.

Bronze bells clang, clang. He smiles. The market stirs.

He's wary of Rome   with its ubiquitous informers,
that ermine horde of envious academics,   vicious
slave catchers,   barbers, alchemists,   bold whores,
timid nobles,   monks assiduous and ambitious,
Macedonian muleteers,   tanners,   drapers,
merchants hawking wine,   snuff,   fish pies;
astrologers,   jugglers,   wheelwrights, coopers,
Slavic soldiers-for-hire,   Spanish spies—

Determined, too,   to circumvent those sly priests
Who   in their abstruse numerical codes
scheme   to betray him   to the Inquisition
("a nest of vipers   among ten thousand   toads"),
Galileo publishes   in Venice   his little book,
The Starry Messenger. The closed globe of thought explodes.

II

VISION

Thou seest the constellations in the deep & wondrous Night;
They rise in order and continue their immortal courses . . .

William Blake, *Milton*

1

"I've discovered four planets never before known—
not," Galileo writes, "since the dawn of time."

In *The Starry Messenger* he sketches their motion.

2

He reports the Milky Way is not a vaporous river.
Nor is it a stream of milk from Hera's breast.

Nor is it the spine of the sky—the pale backbone
of the black beast whose belly is our home.

Nor is it the ancient route of a raven's flight
through a night of snow.

Nor is it the path of souls descending from heaven to earth.
Nor the spirits of the dead departing to the other world.

3

In watercolors he has painted the first maps of the moon
oddly luminous and dim.

For all his faults, passion and wonder are immense in him:
"A beautiful and delightful sight!" he writes of the moon's body.

"Its surface is not polished; but rough, irregular,
like the face of the earth—

mountainous, abounding in deep valleys, plunging chasms."

4

The stars no longer are transported by angels
who hang them from the vault of night.

5

Earth is forever
spinning upon its axis
orbiting the sun.

6

"This short-sighted charlatan
Galileo is guilty
of flagrant blasphemy,
impiety,
and a pernicious
heresy," two
Dominican clerics cry:

"By Satan driven
to deny
Aristotle and Ptolemy
in the dark
sanctuary of night
he has spied
upon the heavens!"

Because he confirmed
Copernicus's vision:
the planets revolving
about the sun.

Because he discovered
the moons of Jupiter
circling
the mother planet.

Because he added, then,
eighty stars
(previously unseen)
to the belt of Orion.

Because he bestowed
a flock of three
dozen new stars
upon the seven Pleiades.

7

"Let our minds examine,"
he implores us,
"what the mind's eye sees."

Because he believes
perspective is a useful illusion
deftly it lifts the veil

from the soul
and we see all that happens
in one world happens in the other—

Painting the *Crucifixion*
Tintoretto urges us to trust our eyes
to guide us

under the storm-tossed trees
to the bald hilltop
and they spare us nothing:

Not the princes, priests, merchants;
even the powerful are curious—
at a distance they sit their mounts.

Not the whirl of spectators, which includes
the complaisant dog
watching the man with the spade.

Not the two soldiers rolling dice,
six laborers binding a thief to a cross,
the circle of mourners collapsed beneath their grief.

Look—here is Jesus hanging by his hands.
Stakes are driven through his hands and feet.
A soldier prepares to stab him with a spear.

We see Jesus' head is bowed.
Too late at the foot of the cross
a woman strains to hear his last words.

From his throat a cry
has been torn.
It chills the air we breathe.

Look—
though the worst is done
there is no limit to our fears.

The vault of heaven itself lies broken.
Lightning is about to strike
from the yellow sky

which appears over Golgotha.
Its gleam yields
little warmth

on the wild hill
where men and women weeping
embrace each other

without shame.
This is how we join the just
and the unjust.

This is how we find our way
in the world men have made
as if we were gods.

When dusk deepens   over the sea   and the sky
shimmers   the long-striding day   with its sacred
sense of possibility   departs.   As the last light
withdraws   into an Adriatic evening   the woman steps
deliberately over   drenched blue stones.   Spilling from
mollusk shells,   washing out of swollen   sea anemone,
a coarse sand,   bronze and black,   swirls at her feet.

The man beside her   sees   even the stragglers
among the gulls are rising   scrabbling   into the air
before he understands   it is absence   that sustains
their cries and loss   is not the end of love.
Walking down the shore   they trail the gulls
expecting night   to overtake them   but the birds
wander out to sea   where   in a single thought

they settle among the waves   rocking to sleep
as the hour continues   darkening   within
its burnished border   while it unfolds   a plush
beauty almost   beyond belief   like the robe
of a scandalous pontiff   seen for what it is
and still it is so   elaborately spread
before them   upon the water in purple splendor.

In a notebook seized prior to his execution by agents of the
Inquisition, Giordano Bruno asserts a limitless universe and
questions the reliability of all optical perception . . .

Because each of us is a creature of the unfathomable
God, we are formed, sweet friends, in the likeness
of that exquisitely inventive sovereign
Lord who (unutterably alone)
occupies one vast
Heaven among the hundred million heavens.

For just as you and I are a world within the world
so, too, many galaxies—stellar dominions—must grow
like fires that flare up in a black and endless forest

(for such is the forest of the night):

conflagrations which ignite and so acquire
(every one according to its nature)
a serviceable shape

only to die
a slowly blazing death
beyond our comprehension

but never beyond
the mind of the one
Creator who brought them forth.

O, my clever companions, tell me:
How is the immense mystery
of a truly solitary

God to be revealed
or refuted?

Honor our striving if not our success . . .

For within us arise walls more formidable than stone or mortar.
Within the prison of each person exist many cells
inhabited by—would you say—angels or demons?
Are we not then the agents of our own doom or bliss?

What might I confess
that I dare not
act out
in the dusky light of every thought?

For in the mind of any man or woman dwells
not a trickster
but a diligent
reverent
and cunning magician.

For if the eye shares its curvature
with the everywhere bending earth
then indeed our slightest observation
(like the most intricate sighting)
requires infinite adjustment—

Imagine,
my brothers, my sisters,
how little we see clearly and without distortion.

Admonished by the Pope and the Inquisition
—Cardinal Bellarmine, Jesuit theologian—
never again to *think* of the earth in motion

neither to speak nor write of its orbit
about the sun, he feigns obedience. "I
look no more to the sky," he tells his daughter

who fears for his life. And his soul. "Earth
yields marvels enough." A politic lie.
Though in a year of sullen isolation

Galileo patiently grinding
his finest lens
has perfected the microscope.

"Closer, now—
Consider
what monsters swim in every drop of water!"

III

INTERLUDE

Love is the highest religion.

Ibn 'Arabi

1

Wet fevers. Pustulant sores. Swollen limbs.
"Is this the Almighty Judgment of our sins?"

While Jews are shaved bald and scrubbed with vinegar
High Mass is performed in the public square.

2

Patients are fed a cedar syrup; arsenic;
figs, oil from the meat of a female snake.

They're bled. Leeches are applied to wounds. Also
eviscerated pigeons. Or a red-hot coal.

3

Survivors gather gauzes, boots, soiled sheets,
gowns and shirts, then burn them on smoking grates.

Beneath the clouded sun a lone gondolier
rides the canal, rowing through the putrid air.

4

When the living loot the luxuriant homes of the dead
they cart off carpets, draperies; never a bed.

5

A veiled silence pervades the previously
gossipy silk shops of the Mercerie.

In their cages—has everyone sailed away?—
blinded songbirds warble night and day.

6

The blackening body of the wine merchant afloat
in the lagoon nudges the dock like a tethered boat.

7

Down a narrow corridor wild dogs attack
each other, snarling, jaws snapping in the dark.

Stacks of bloated corpses congest the streets
where grave diggers hawk their labor—family rates!

Love is not longing it is action—
The six novices in the monastery garden know this

and it makes them furious.
They swear between their teeth.

On their knees
in soil wet with last night's rain

to weed the bean rows
with no breakfast this morning but bitter coffee.

In anger the six hiss like a swarm of black bees
while they pull the weeds.

Herons thrive in Ostia where no ship sails
into harbor. Fishnets fray. Unknot. Return
to stray hemp—threads for nests. Once a port fails

to satisfy the Roman soul, merchants spurn
its market. More marsh than river, the Tiber sprawls
before us. Frogs roil the shallows. Here, we learn,

the Emperor Hadrian wept. Among wine halls
Augustine remembered his lost life. Here,
down a wharf thick with shops, makeshift stalls,

Pope Urban led his blind astrologer.
Rain threatens and a homing heron calls
its mate. Together they approach the shore

where a resplendent shrine, neglected, falls
to ruin: while the last mosaics break
the lusty gods cavort across these walls—

Noon finds them lying shattered in the wake
of a black squall. Already summer trails
Hadrian into history. Herons rake

the marsh. At dusk they roost among the scales
on the docks of Ostia, where no ship sails.

The Madonna of Purgatory
holds no child in her arms.
(A scandal—the model
was the sculptor's mistress,
a bold woman familiar
with backroom beds, dank
studios.) She stands alone
upon this hillside the city
can live without, among serried
pines which shade the outcrop
of ancient rock. You notice
her stone form appears at home
here: head bowed as if
she's listening for a favorite
birdsong. The call of a fox.
Her cloak brown like the worn soil
beneath her feet. To all
her arms are barely extended—
a reserve which suggests
every breath is our last
effort not to scream. Eyes
neither gentle nor kind;
a forbearing gaze tested
by centuries of betrayal.
If our hope is in her hands
what dream of deliverance
draws us to this place? Where pines
cast cave-like shadows while
fresh-cut boughs surround
her shrine with a wild fragrance.

1

Into the torch-lit square
come spangled timbrels,
the rising thrum
of a Spanish guitar,
three burnished horns
and an eel-skin drum.

Hundreds in costume dance
in their wake—the prison
cook flaunts the billowing
mauve sleeves of a countess.
Mad boars. Mermaids. Marching
bears. Priests, street-
thieves. Merchants' wives.
Pimps, jugglers, acrobats.

2

A jet-haired gypsy
rider—how young
she looks!—tucks
her head; flings
both feet skyward,
naked belly taut
but slender legs
waggling, sustaining
her uncertain balance,
palms upon the tawny
back of her pony.

3

The courtesan confined
by her ponderous black
robe—tonight she's Chief
Magistrate—frees one
arm from its velvet fold,
shaking her tambourine.

The bearded bride, so coy
beside her buxom groom—
a blacksmith and his wife.
His white gown almost splits;
she traipses in borrowed
boots, trousers. They kiss
and share a belly laugh.

Behind the blind mule
wearing a bishop's miter
four whores stroll
happily
bare-breasted
scattering flowers.

4

Milanese armor gleams
no less than saddlery tooled
in silver. At open tents
fish for sale. Fresh bread.
Piping little pigs battle
for scraps. Caged birds
entertain us with trills.
Wineskins sway overhead.

A cat, stretching, rubs the lavender leg
of the Grand Duchess of Tuscany.

A prostitute in a disheveled dress
accompanies the bald courtier
bearing a mirror (hers or his?)
in which he admires the fading image
of a middle-aged Narcissus.

When the cat strolls away
it's abruptly caught
up, nuzzled, by
a frightened boy who steals purses.

5

Their tunics trimmed
with ivy, two
slender youths
play wooden flutes.

6

Wine wakens the ardent fake
Franciscan abbot—by day
a devout bureaucrat—
to her animal nature:
this two-legged lioness.
As they undo her dun-
colored costume down
to undulating hips
her tail's a lithe
length of rope which
twitches with glee.

"There's nothing make-
believe about me,"
she purrs, a feline
forepaw prodding
his crotch: "Watch."

7

Before any hint of rain
when the air thickens
it smells of horse
shit, fish, pigs,
incense and wine:
a dense cloud that gathers
over walkways twisting
among the vendors' tents.

8

Step inside. Shadowy
lean-to stalls
ask for our souls—
What do we yearn to see?

The Pope's young bride
is the pouting gypsy
girl who rode a pony
standing on her hands.

But the monkey-boy!
The horned giraffe!
A fire-eating Turk!
The fabulous Minotaur of Crete?

Under her flickering lamp
an onyx-eyed Veronese
crone casts fortunes
in the entrails of geese.

Couples gather armfuls of straw
into a corner the crowd
chooses to ignore;
in the dark we ask no names
but shed costumes
and masks
to discover each other.

9

Distant thunder. The last revelers
wander off; sink
down in
inextricable passageways
together and alone.

Dawn brings its half-light
to the abandoned square.
Tents are unstaked,
rolled, taken up
as torches gutter out
and horses shake in their sleep

while upon us all
the morning rain
promising
not pardon but mercy
murmurs its blessing.

IV

AN UNQUIET MIND

The century is dark; it cannot see the sky. The stars are cloaked by clouds. There is no glow; the sun has disappeared in darkness, and the moon is blood.

Tommaso Campanella

Galileo Visits His Mistress while Her Son Sleeps,
Dreaming of His Own Death

1

Sweltering Venice is still his pleasure palace
though Papal agents lurk about its market—
And yesterday he recognized two young priests
prowling the city archives, posing as scholars.
He prides himself on unmasking every disguise.
"Yet these witless eunuchs persist," he laments:
"Oh, the languorous and patient impotence of spies!"

Seated by the arched window of her drawing room,
the woman who insists she is not a courtesan
strokes the severe pleats in her scarlet gown.

2

Late afternoon. Among the market stalls
reeking of oregano, a butchered boar,
deer skinned and salted, quail, pickled eels, wheels
of parmesan, goats' blood, garlic, fish oil,
the boy sleeps fitfully on a straw mat,
muttering as an indigo shade consumes his legs.
Around his neck hangs a talisman: two teeth
from a white rat to ward off the Black Death.

Early in his dream his mother searches
the market for him, sobbing, calling his name.
Bulbous sores fester over his body
swollen and gradually blackening

like the others, the dead and the living
dead deposited on the cobbled *calle*
abutting the canals, before the grave
diggers with their ravenous carts arrive.

With the stench of death in his nostrils he wakes,
shaking off the rags of that fading dream.
Sitting now, shuddering, the boy discovers
a keen-eyed monk squatting on calloused heels.
Rising, the old cleric extends his hand
to the trembling youth. He offers him almonds,
sun-dried dates. Asking, as he walks him home,
"Your mother's friend—you've heard how he curses Rome?"

3

Galileo, served his third cup of wine, drinks it down,
wiping his lips with a disinfected cloth
so hot it steams; an old precaution. Never
relax your vigilance. Vermin. Inquisitors.
"Wretches! Such cold fish! If only their wrath
were seasoned with a little lust. No! No—
their shame is that they desire nothing
in all God's world but my disgrace. And then my death."

Idly the woman rises from her window seat.
Still she lingers beyond his reach.
He'll charm her with his candor . . .

"I tell no tender lies," he boasts.
"One day you might try," she suggests.

Stepping onto the balcony he praises her bougainvillea,
there, where it tumbles, spilling its velvety crimson
bounty between them. The breeze caught in the curtain
sighs. Rose blossoms float in a cerulean bowl
as she extends her arms to embrace the twilight hour.
The day sinks into memory. The dusk is in her eyes.

22 ★ *Six Fragments from Johannes Kepler's Last Letter to Galileo*

1

My dear and distant friend—

As my mind, a troubled stream,
subsides from turbulence to form,
I write to you once again
in the pain of my solitude.
Tell me, please, my offense.

Do I shame you?

Soldiers occupy my house.
A guardsman with a grizzly beard
died of his wounds in my bed.

You might think me mad.

2

Forgive me. No doubt you're aware
I'm said to be dangerous.
(I—the least of men!)
By ill-repute unstable, thus
a threat to Rome *and* Reform.
While the same mouths claim
I'm the merest fool. Witless,
dithering, slow. Perhaps.
But how can both be so?

Rumor spreads, fatal as a fever.
Do I witness sounds unheard of
in the sky? Hues foreign
to the earth beneath our feet?
To speak the truth, my master,
these tales frighten me to death!

3

Our books will burn—the bindings
yielding, their careful pages
curling, blackening; moth-like
wings of soot up-swirling. I
dare not attempt to rescue
my thoughts. I cannot reach them
through the cursing and the smoke
clouding all the square.

4

Your turn will come.
Be bold. As I am
not. Yet beware.

5

However earnestly we strive
the future is ruthless—
none survive it
and our only guide is love.

6

Like all men who think, I struggle
against my nature. Wherein
I acknowledge what I hear
or dream is but the ghost
of those heavenly harmonics
that move the mind to dance:
Why not, then, call it music
and admit our souls are lost?

More circumspect than hunters setting
traps in the tawny Tuscan hills,
clerics plotted their steps:
which witnesses required torture?
All the while accumulating
evidence for the Inquisitor's file.

Forsaking caution, Galileo
acknowledged each enemy
unnerved him. He grew brash,
contemptuous—the child
he'd been before the world
discovered him. True,
he'd sought preferment. Who
has not? No matter—he
was appalled by authority
unless it favored him . . .

Among faithful supporters
he counted three emissaries
to the Papal Court. Also
a prince. A Minister
of State, no less. And, yes,
the Grand Duke of Tuscany.

Behind bejeweled fingers
they grinned, they tittered,
to hear their friend—his cup
filled to spilling—propose
his toast to progress; then

declare the Pope, "A dupe,
a dullard, a simpleton.
A worm. A brass-brained dolt.
A sheep. A braying ass
spooked by its own shadow."

Clearly he feared no man
now. No—not even
pious Pope Urban
who strangled songbirds
in the Vatican garden
when they disturbed him.

24 * Galileo Speaks with God on a Midsummer Night of Shimmering Stars

1

The moon is late and still the hour shines.
Cedars shudder in their blackness.
From far off a faint jingling.
"Do you hear our tower bells?
The wind plays them like a timbrel."

2

Planets appear to glow with their own life.
The fabric of the heavens at any moment
might become a glimmering tapestry.
Truth—to an unquiet mind—is never quite enough.

3

"The stars blaze above us.
How did you know we would love them so?"

4

He wishes to ask a wicked question
but his courage fails him:
Why offer us such beauty—distant
bells tremulous in the high wind;
the diffident dance of the great trees;
this wonder that steals our breath away—
and certain death?

5

How long has he lived alone?
He believes he cannot know
how to cherish a woman
beyond his passion
for her. Always
fearing she'll leave him.
The dread of an unwanted child.

6

"I understand my duty.
But you have formed a darkness so vast and lovely
it hurts my heart."

With the restless shuttling sound
of a spirited loom at work
the night wind turns the sky to silk.

1

Charged with heresy—to answer the accusation
Galileo is summoned
before the Holy Office of the Inquisition.

The fire of sciatic pain
without relief
from hip to calf

renders him incapable of sitting his horse.
Or riding in a coach upholstered in hand-worked leather;
goose-down pillows propped upon a small couch.

No—he must be transported from Florence to Rome
on a litter borne by mules; the team driven
by two burly men who dare not speak his name—

The charge itself is proof of his crime.

2

However hungry he may be
however he thirsts
for the local wine
they avoid each village

that flies the black flag
over its whitewashed gate.
Each sullen city
punished by the plague.

Pausing outside the wall
he's struck by the stillness—
so many suffering souls
and not one voice.

Gasping
he inhales their stench—
Wood fires and putrid flesh.
Pus-sopped rags. The dung pile.

No turning back. At noon
the sun is weak as water.
Above thatched or tile
rooftops undulates a shroud of smoke.

3

Tossing and twisting
in a half-sleep
beside the starlit road.
Arising stiff and sore.

Taking stock—he's seventy.
A proud man of too much bulk
and failing sight. Weary,
frightened, he expects little pity.

And no rest
until they reach the Eternal City.

4

His prison is an apartment already of ample size
further enlarged by a full-length mirror
in which he views the terror in his eyes.

He paces the parquet floor.
Behind drawn draperies the windows are latched.
Four guards stand posted at the door.

5

"What do we *want?*
Confess.
Then recant."

Or he can harbor no hope
of returning to his home.
Not even deformed by torture. Not ever.

6

Kept awake forty hours
without water
howling in the dark

by day falling mute
suffering depression

dizziness
shitting with fear

he is led unshackled into the Cellar Chamber.
A priest at his side.
A candle guttering in every corner.

The priest   a practiced guide   through the Cellar Chamber
deplores sudden force   but admits to a trace of guile:
"Pressure and mere patience   accomplish much.   Do I
surprise you?   Brother and sister in spirit, remember.

This pair of clamps crushes   a heretic's legs so slowly,
—*di grado in grado*—"   A sober gaze fixed all the while
upon his guest.   "Should he stifle that blood-stained cry
he has time to recant   by God's mercy to redeem his soul."

Candlelight flickers.   The room falls breathless; still.
Touching his tunic   he offers Galileo an enigmatic smile.

1

"Torture," the priest advises him, "rarely is meant to punish.
At worst we may wish to coerce a confession.
Often our purpose is to correct error
or reverse an impious opinion.

However, to open the eyes of the soul may prove
a painful task. A dreadful discipline at best.
Yet think of these as instruments of salvation—
surely the goal is worth its cost."

Pincers recline in a bed of coals—
the branding iron, too, is white hot.
Lips must be blistered to warn of blasphemy.
The forehead singed for sacrilege, the mind's revolt.

The serrated knife removes idle fingers or thumb.
Or an offending tongue.
Covering the culprit's head for however long,
a sailcloth sack, secured at the neck, leaves no mark.

Galileo learns how gradually the strappado
(his faithful guide esteems it
"the queen of torments")
severs a man's shoulders.

How the accused is bound to the rack
and its greased levers grind,
unceasing under his screams,
shattering both kneecaps.

His groin ruptures.
His ribcage cracks twice
before his spine straightens
then snaps.

2

Released, revived,
he's lashed
to a donkey;
driven through the street.

In a square the jeering mob
awaits the sinner
at the tarred pole,
the tinder pile
where twelve guards
with pikes poised,
twelve with sabers,
wheel and march—

black boots drumming
on the cobbles.

The crowd quiets—
the hooded friar
dipping his torch
ignites the pyre.

The first tall flame.
How it suspires—
like the high dark
wind in the pines.

3

Memory and imagination; regardless of our intention,
how often each gate opens to the same garden.

4

Galileo at thirty-six had seen, here in Rome, one night
in the Piazza dei Fiori, in the Square of Flowers,
Giordano Bruno, rolling his outraged blue eyes
as the clamp was pried from his jaw,
the spike from his tongue,
should he wish to recant
with his last breath.
In vain.
        Only curses
and a bubble of blood
ballooned from his mouth,
spattering on the stones.

Limbs flailing—that futile lurch
before he was chained to the stake and burned alive.

5

As ever, his fear
of pain afflicts
the astronomer with chills and sweats.

Struggling to stand fast
in the tidal pull
of a fainting spell,
he shivers with fever.

A quivering penitent. No need to preach
pieties about the Pope's authority.
Still, after revisiting the rack,
a calm hand at his elbow for support,
he is shown the executioner's wadded torch.

In the plain white robe of a penitent
the astronomer is led into the trial hall,
its narrow window frosted under a low ceiling.
One bronze crucifix on the scrubbed wall.

Imprisonment has further blurred his dim
eyesight. Daylight so dazzles him
he staggers to his chair.
On the oak table, a calf-bound bible.

His inquisitors sit robed in black
and white: two Dominican monks
who call themselves the Hounds of God.
Though Galileo knows the breed—

attack dogs, unrelenting, grim—
their zeal this morning alarms him:
"We hunt heretics, make no mistake;
we pursue the impious to the ends of the earth."

No need to dwell upon the dungeon
housing the rack. Leather cudgels
that bruise without breaking skin.
Cuffs, leg-clamps, pincers, cinches.

The perpetually smoking bed of coals.
The surgeon's table; his saw-toothed knife.
They trust his memory of these
is bright as blood and will suffice.

His crime is that his books have taught
a radical displacement of the earth
from the center of God's universe
into an orbit about the sun

in one of many galaxies.
There is no defense for this sin.
He must first renounce his theories
then beg forgiveness on his knees.

"You, sir, will satisfy our hunger
for compliance," instructs the elder
monk. "No doubt your exploration
of the Cellar Chamber acquainted you

with our Instruments of Truth."
Flinching, the prisoner averts his gaze
and for the first time he focuses
on their scribe. This frail functionary

seated near the door is a nun;
the same order as his daughter.
Not cowled but hooded like a man.
At last grasping his situation,

he absorbs the stillness in the room;
servants of the Lord they may be,
but they are masters of humiliation.
If they deliver him to the dungeon,

this woman, his daughter's likeness, surely
will attend his torment and transcribe
his screams upon her heart. How can he
not recant? They are waiting.

A wintry blast rattles the window;
the first snow? Legs twitching
in pain he whimpers like a child,
then abandons himself to weeping.

Upon rising he dries his eyes
with the heel of his trembling hand.
An old man afraid of torture,
ashamed the solitary nun

must witness his tears, his disgrace,
he kneels before their slippered feet
to deny the earth its orbit
and the significance of the sun.

This morning, sipping a caffe black as oil,
he received the Pope's reply. Tonight he writes
his beloved daughter: "Though I'd sought only
to see—and say—what is actual, and real,

I lied to spare my life. Yes, at what price?
My soul is damned. My poor books condemned.
Dearest, tell Papa now, quite honestly,
have all my studies brought your spirit peace?"

Autumn rain at the window fills his room
with a rhythm almost restful. The pond
rises in the dark. Tomorrow, surely,
his horses will drink from a swollen stream.

This—that these creatures shouldn't thirst—matters
more than his own hunger. This merciful
benefit of burgeoning marshes, wells,
and creeks; wherever the water gathers.

"Hope alone heals. Like rare rain. I see more
clearly your devotion since my eyes dim.
Love, we live so alike. You within
your convent house. The armed guards at my door.

How the almighty God must weep—or laugh—
over my folly. I may teach no truth.
And yet I might—a ghost awaiting death—
guide you to discern it within yourself."

1

His sentence—life imprisonment—is commuted
to house arrest. Confined to the hilltop
villa near his daughter's convent, he writes
until his sight fails him. Welcomes visits
from Milton. From Thomas Hobbes. One woman
weaves intelligence with her tender humor.
She reads to him and he adores her. Until
this moment no one has ever troubled him
with kindness. "My fault—who pets a wild pig?"

She answers him with laughter. Then gossip.
He loves it—always has—plucked ripe from court.

Blind, he paces a gabled room, halting
at the latched window which overlooks
a leafless orchard. Plodding down the path,
his favorite mule follows a field hand home.
He hears its bell clanging, clanging. So like
what? Venice? Yes, years ago. Early
morning. The call to the marketplace. Leaving
its chill, twilight ebbs from the windowpane.
He settles his bulk on the bed, gasping for breath.
Fingers pluck a horse blanket over his smock.

2

Though the age died when he was brought to trial,
upon his death his argument made its way
across Europe. Beyond guarded borders
it was whispered. Tested. The results sheltered
in private libraries. Advanced in learned societies.
And—this would not astonish him—in the secret
teachings of Jesuit fathers in China and Japan.

3

Will we learn too late to love? On one small
satellite of the sun the mind imagines
its origin: from interstellar clouds
of dust, solar wind, daylight, earth
itself struck by lightning, soothed by rain,
consciousness emerges. He brought us this
vision of the universe—a process ongoing,
accessible to the thought of man or woman.

In nature are we not bonded to one another?
Stars, atoms, grass, water, soil.
Doves that disturb the peace of the vineyard.
Two hawks circling a sleeping hill. In time
we learn that each question is a prayer—
will we learn to love each day without fear?
Already his plum orchard standing bare
in the dead of winter prepares its purple bloom
while dawn illuminates a silent room.

Acknowledgments

I wish to acknowledge, with thanks, the editors of the following publications in which poems from *The Starry Messenger* sequence appeared, sometimes in a different form:

Edge City Review: "Upon Learning His Appeal for a Pardon Is Denied"; *Ekphrasis:* "Herons," "On Trial," and "Tintoretto" (reprinted); *Hellas:* "Venice: The Morning Market Opens"; *Mobius:* "His Fondness for Animals, His Fear of Pain, His Fabulous Appetite"; *Natural Bridge:* "A Cautionary Tour of the Cellar Chamber"; *the new renaissance:* "Carnevale"; *New York Times:* "Herons" (reprinted); *Northern Contours:* "What Monsters"; *Pivot:* "Ambition," "The Black Death Visits Venice," "Galileo Visits His Mistress while Her Son Sleeps, Dreaming of His Own Death," and "Heresy"; *River Oak Review:* "The Astronomer's Childhood and Early Youth" and "The Whispering City"; *Sewanee Review:* "Authority," "The Madonna of Purgatory," "Six Fragments from Johannes Kepler's Last Letter to Galileo," "Wary of Rome," and "Writing in Her Diary, His Daughter Welcomes the First Spring Rain Falling in the Hills"; *Sierra Journal:* "Desire"; *Wild Duck Review:* "In the Monastery Garden"; *Windhover:* "Charting the Planets" and "Tintoretto"; *RUNES, A Review of Poetry:* "Adriatic Evening"; *Wormwood Review* (Storrs, Conn.): "Herons."

Thanks also for the Allen Tate Prize awarded for the following poems, which appeared in *Sewanee Review:* "Portrait of Galileo as a Young Man," vol. 107, no. 2; "The Death of Galileo" and "What the Mind's Eye Sees," vol. 108, no. 1; "Galileo Speaks with God on a Midsummer Night of Shimmering Stars" and "Stellar Dominions," vol. 108, no. 3.

The quotation by Tommaso Campanella appears in Helen Langdon's *Carravagio: A Life* (Farrar, Straus and Giroux).

For their generosity of spirit I wish to thank the many people who have expressed interest in these poems. I appreciate the assistance given so readily by Marvin Bell, Daniel Hoffman, and X. J. Kennedy. I'm especially grateful to George Core for his thoughtfulness, his sensibility, and his concern for the poems. The time required to complete the book has been enriched, as ever, by the companionship and understanding of my wife, Carol.

GEORGE KEITHLEY is the author of eight books of poetry, including *The Midnight Train*, *Living Again*, and *Song in a Strange Land*. His epic poem, *The Donner Party*, was a Book-of-the-Month Club Selection and was adapted as a stage play and an opera. His poems, stories, and essays have appeared in the *New York Times*, *Harper's*, and *American Poetry Review*, and have earned numerous awards, including a Pushcart Prize and the DiCastagnola Award from the Poetry Society of America. Born in Chicago and educated at Duke, Stanford, and the University of Iowa, he has been a visiting writer in Russia. He and his wife live in California.